Religions of the World
Hinduism

Sue Penney

Heinemann
LIBRARY

www.heinemann.co.uk/library

Visit our website to find out more information about Heinemann Library books.

To order:

☎ Phone 44 (0) 1865 888066

🖹 Send a fax to 44 (0) 1865 314091

💻 Visit the Heinemann Bookshop at www.heinemann.co.uk/library to browse our catalogue and order online.

First published in Great Britain by Heinemann Library, Halley Court, Jordan Hill, Oxford OX2 8EJ
a division of Reed Educational and Professional Publishing Ltd.
Heinemann is a registered trademark of Reed Educational & Professional Publishing Ltd.

OXFORD MELBOURNE AUCKLAND JOHANNESBURG BLANTYRE GABORONE
IBADAN PORTSMOUTH (NH) USA CHICAGO

Designed by Ken Vail Graphic Design
Originated by Universal
Printed by Wing King Tong in Hong Kong.

ISBN 0 431 14955 0

06 05 04 03 02
10 9 8 7 6 5 4 3 2 1

British Library Cataloguing in Publication Data

Penney, Sue
Hinduism. – (Religions of the world)
1.Hinduism – Juvenile literature
1.Title
294.5

Acknowledgments
The Publishers would like to thank the following for permission to reproduce photographs:
Andes Press Agency/Carlos Reyes-Manzo, pp. 5, 10, 16, 22, 28, 29, 30, 35, 38, 39, 42; Ann & Bury Peerless,
pp. 7, 12, 17, 20, 37, 43; Christine Osborne Pictures, pp. 6, 8, 9, 21, 23, 26, 36, 40, 41; Circa Photos Library,
pp. 11/John Smith, 14/Bipin J. Mistry, 25/William Holtby, 32/Robyn Beeche; FLPA/E. & D. Hosking, p. 4;
Hutchison, pp. 24, 27, 31, 33; Mary Evans Picture Library, p. 13; Phil & Val Emmett, p. 34.

Cover photograph reproduced with permission of Hutchison Picture Library.

Our thanks to Philip Emmett for his comments in the preparation of this book.

Every effort has been made to contact copyright holders of any material reproduced in this book. Any
omissions will be rectified in subsequent printings if notice is given to the Publisher.

Words appearing in the text in bold, **like this**, are explained in the Glossary.

Contents

Dates: In this book, dates are followed by the letters BCE (Before Common Era) or CE (Common Era). This is instead of using BC (Before Christ) and AD (*Anno Domini*, meaning In the year of our Lord), which is a Christian system. The date numbers are the same in both systems.

Introducing Hinduism

Hinduism is the oldest of the world's religions. It is so old that no one really knows when it began, or how it began.

Sanatan dharma

Different Hindus may believe quite different things, even though they all follow the religion of Hinduism. Most Hindus do not use the word 'Hinduism'. They call their religion **Sanatan dharma**. This means '**eternal** truths'. Eternal means something that lasts for ever.

▲ *Banyan trees spread their roots from the main tree trunk. Some people say that this could be a symbol of Hinduism.*

Facts about Hinduism

- *Hinduism began about 5000 years ago in northern India.*
- *Hindus worship Brahman (God) through different gods and goddesses.*
- *Hindus worship in temples, and at **shrines** in their homes and other places.*
- *The oldest Hindu holy books are called the Vedas.*
- *About 800 million people in India are Hindus. This is more than 80 per cent of the people in India.*
- *Hindus also live in many other countries. There are about one million Hindus in the USA and 360,000 Hindus in the UK.*

Hindus believe that their religion teaches things which are true, which have always been true and which will always be true. These truths are written down in the Hindu holy books. The first holy books are called the **Vedas**.

What do Hindus believe?

Hindus believe that there is one Great Power. Many Hindus would say that this power can be called God. The Hindu name for the Great Power is **Brahman**. Most Hindus say that Brahman is not a person, and not male or female, but 'it'. Brahman is everywhere, and in everything. Most Hindus say that this power can be seen most easily through gods and goddesses.

▲ *These Hindus are worshipping at a temple in the UK.*

Hindus believe that everything has a **soul**, called the **atman**. A soul is the part of a person which lives on after the person's body has died. They believe that when someone dies, their atman moves on. It may go to live in another person, or it may live in an animal or a plant. This is called **reincarnation**. Where the atman goes depends on how the person has lived in this life. Hindus believe that this happens again and again. They believe that when someone becomes good enough, it stops happening. Then the atman can become part of Brahman. This is what Hindus aim for.

Aum

The **symbol** for Hinduism spells the world **Aum**. It is said 'Ah-oo-m'. Hindus believe that this is a holy sound. They believe that it is a way of describing Brahman.

Gods and goddesses

Hinduism has thousands of different gods and goddesses. Hindus may worship any of them. Three of the most well-known gods are Vishnu, Shiva and Ganesha.

Vishnu

Hindus believe that Vishnu has come to earth nine times. Each time, he came when the earth was in danger. He came to protect it. The two most important times were when he came as the god Rama, and then as the god Krishna. Krishna is a very popular god for Hindus.

Shiva

Shiva is worshipped by about 25 per cent of all Hindus. Hindus believe that Shiva is in charge of life and death, and of good and evil. This is why statues of Shiva show him with at least four hands. He is often shown dancing, and one of his names is Lord of the Dance. Hindus believe that his dance is the energy which keeps the universe moving.

Ganesha

Ganesha has an elephant's head. In the family of gods, he is Shiva's son. Hindus believe that Shiva cut off Ganesha's head by mistake, and gave him an elephant's head instead. For Hindus, Ganesha is the god of learning and good luck. Hindus who are beginning something new often pray to him. They ask that what they are starting will be successful.

A statue of Lakshmi, the goddess of beauty and wealth, with Ganesha, the god of learning.

Why do Hindus pray to statues?

*Hindus believe that they cannot understand **Brahman**, the Great Power. They believe that they are more likely to worship Brahman properly if they worship gods and goddesses who they can understand. There are many stories about the gods and their families which help people to understand them. The statues in temples and **shrines** help people to concentrate when they worship.*

The Mother Goddess

Hindus also believe in goddesses. The most important goddess is the Mother Goddess. She has many different names which show different parts of her character. She is Durga and Kali, who are frightening and fierce. She is also Parvati and Saraswati, who are kind and gentle. As Lakshmi, she is Vishnu's wife and the goddess of beauty. Hindus pray to Lakshmi because they hope she will bring them luck, especially with money.

As Kali, the Mother Goddess is frightening and cruel.

The early days of Hinduism

These ruins are from people who lived in the Indus Valley about 5000 years ago.

No one knows exactly when Hinduism began, but it was about 5000 years ago. It started gradually among people who lived in what is now called north India. This place is known as the Indus Valley. In the twentieth century CE, archaeologists found things that belonged to these people. They showed that these ancient people were very organized, and that they worshipped a Mother Goddess and a bull.

You can find the places mentioned in this book on the map on page 44.

In about 1500 BCE, this part of India was taken over by people from the country now called Iran. The people from Iran worshipped gods of the sun, moon and stars. As years passed, the two different kinds of worship mixed. People began worshipping other gods as well as their own. This went on for about 1000 years.

Changes in Hinduism

During the fourth and third centuries BCE, Buddhism became popular in India. Many Hindus became **Buddhists**. Hindu teachers saw that Hinduism needed to change. It needed to become more organized. The teachers began writing down the Hindu holy books. They spent a lot of time teaching, and Hinduism became more popular again.

The Moghuls

After about 1100 CE, **Moghuls** ruled India for about 300 years. They were **Muslims**, and they did not like the way Hindus worshipped. Many Indian people became Muslim, and Hinduism became less popular again. Many Hindu temples were pulled down.

Recent history

The world changed very quickly during the nineteenth and twentieth centuries CE. Hindu leaders had to show that Hinduism was still important. Many famous Hindu teachers worked during this time. Today, most people living in India are Hindu, and Hindus live in many different countries throughout the world.

Hinduism is now a mixture of many different beliefs. Hindus say what matters is that people find the truth for themselves.

Hare Krishna

*One of the best-known groups of Hindus in the world today is called the International Society for Krishna Consciousness (ISKCON). It teaches that people need to wake up to what they really are. They do this by repeating words called a **mantra**. The mantra is 'Hare Krishna'. Followers of this group believe that everything they do is an offering to the god Krishna.*

9

The caste system

The **caste** system is the way that people in India have lived for thousands of years. People are divided into groups, called **varnas**. There are four main varnas.

The four varnas

The highest varna are **Brahmins**. They are priests. The second group are **Kshatriyas**. They are soldiers and princes. The third group are **Vaishyas**. They are shop-keepers, farmers and people who make things. The fourth group are **Shudras**. They are servants for the other three groups. Anyone who does not belong to one of the four main varnas belongs to the **Harijans**. Hindus believe that the Harijans are lower than any other group. They usually do the dirtiest jobs.

Jatis

Over thousands of years, the four main varnas split into many smaller groups, called **jatis** or castes. A person's jati is decided by what jati their family belongs to. Years ago, a jati was decided by a person's job. A son would always do the same job as his father. Girls in those days did not work outside the home. Today, children do not always do the same job as their parents, because they are now often able to go to school, and life is different. However, people still stay in the same jati.

A Hindu priest comes from the varna called Brahmins.

In many Indian villages, people still live in a very traditional way.

Like varnas, some jatis are 'higher' or 'lower' than other jatis. People used to be very strict about not having anything to do with people who came from a lower jati than their own. However, in the past 50 years, things have changed. More people travel away from their home, to live and work. Many change jobs, and people who live in cities meet and talk to other people. Because of this, the rules about jatis cannot be kept so strictly. Many Brahmins are not priests, not all soldiers are Kshatriyas and many people who are not Vaishyas own shops. Even so, most people still know what jati they belong to, and what this means for them and for other people.

Changing the law

In the 1940s, laws were passed in India to try to make different jatis more equal. It is now against the law to treat people differently because of their jati. However, it takes more than laws to change the way that people think. In many villages in India, the caste system is still very strict.

Two Hindu leaders

You can find the places mentioned in this book on the map on page 44.

Ramakrishna (1834–86 CE)

Ramakrishna was a great leader of Hinduism in the nineteenth century. His parents were very poor. When he was 21 years old, Ramakrishna became a priest at a temple to the goddess Kali, near Calcutta in eastern India. He became so involved in the worship that he sometimes went into a **trance**. When he came out of it, he did not know anything about things that had happened around him.

Ramakrishna spent a lot of time caring for other people. He became very famous because he was such a good man. Some of his followers believe that Ramakrishna was so good that he must have been a god himself. When he died in 1886 he left behind many followers to carry on his work.

Mahatma Gandhi (1869–1948 CE)

Mohandas Karamchand Gandhi was born in 1869 in a small town in India. He studied in the UK to become a lawyer. He then went to work in South Africa. Gandhi realized that black people there were treated unfairly, and he began trying to improve their lives. He became a fighter for freedom. He taught about **ahimsa** – fighting for what you believe without using violence.

This statue of Ramakrishna is at the place where he was born.

Gandhi's work in India

When Gandhi went back to India in 1915, he became an important leader. In 1947 he tried to calm the fighting between Hindus and **Muslims** when India was divided to form the new country called Pakistan. Pakistan was created to be a Muslim country and India was mainly a Hindu country. More than six million Muslims left India to live in Pakistan. Five million Hindus moved from Pakistan to India. This was a time of great suffering. There were riots, and thousands of people were killed.

Gandhi's work made him some enemies. On 30 January 1948, Gandhi was shot dead. The man who killed him belonged to a group which disagreed with Gandhi's teachings.

More than three million people took part in Gandhi's funeral procession. Today, Gandhi is remembered by people all over the world. He is respected as a man of peace.

▲ Gandhi used a spinning wheel to show people that work was important.

'Mahatma'

Gandhi is almost always called 'Mahatma', even though his first name was Mohandas. Mahatma was a special title given to him by an Indian poet. It means 'great **soul**'. People use it because it describes what a great man Gandhi was, and that he showed how good can overcome evil.

Hindu holy books

There are many holy books in Hinduism. Some of them are more important than others. Some praise the gods and tell people how to worship. Some help to explain Hinduism to people. Most of the Hindu holy books are written in **Sanskrit**. This is one of the oldest languages in the world. Today, no one speaks or writes Sanskrit in everyday life.

The Hindu holy books are divided into two main groups. The first group is called **shruti**. This means 'heard'. Hindus believe that these words were heard by wise men right at the beginning of Hinduism. The second group is called **smriti**. This means 'remembered'. Hindus believe that these words were passed down through families for hundreds of years until they were written down.

The Vedas

The **Vedas** are the oldest of the Hindu holy books. The word veda means knowledge. Hindus believe that the Vedas contain the most important knowledge, which will never change. The Vedas go back to about 1200 BCE, but they were not written down until about 1400 CE. The most important Veda is the first, which is called the Rig Veda. It contains more than 1000 poems.

*This Hindu priest is reading the Vedas in front of the **shrine** at his home.*

The poems celebrate the Hindu gods of nature. This is part of a poem to the earth goddess Prithivi:

You send us the water-laden cloud, O shining goddess – with your strength you hold the trees firmly in the ground when the lightning flashes and thunder-rain showers from the sky. (Rig Veda 5.84.3)

The Upanishads

The Upanishads are the last part of each Veda. The name Upanishad comes from Sanskrit words which mean 'sit down near'. People used to sit down near teachers who were talking about the Vedas, and learn from them. The Upanishads contain what they learned.

The Laws of Manu

Manu was a wise teacher. No one knows exactly when he lived, but the Laws of Manu were written down by 300 CE. They contain rules about how Hindus should live. They also teach how priests should perform worship.

The Puranas

Puranas means 'olden times'. The Puranas are part of the group of holy books which help to explain the teaching given in the Vedas. They contain many well-known Hindu stories.

A Hindu prayer

*One of the prayers in the Rig Veda is to the sun god Savitri. It is called the Gayatri **mantra**. In Sanskrit it looks like this. Words for it in English are shown below the Sanskrit words.*

ॐ भूर्भुवः स्वः । ॐ तत्सवितुर्वरेण्युं यमों देदस्प धीमहि । भियो यो नः प्रचोदयांत्

We think about the loving light of the god Savitri. May the way he shines like the sun help us to worship.

The Mahabharata and the Ramayana

These children are performing a dance which tells one of the stories from the holy books.

The Mahabharata and the Ramayana are part of the Hindu holy books. They are very long poems. They contain good stories, and they also teach important lessons about the Hindu religion.

The Mahabharata

The Mahabharata is the longest poem in the world. It has more than 100,000 verses! It was written by many different people, over many hundreds of years.

The main story of the Mahabharata is about a quarrel between two royal families. Two cousins quarrel about who should be the ruler of the country. One family tricks the other, and there is a great battle. Before the battle begins, Arjuna, the prince of one of the families, has a conversation with the person driving his chariot. This turns out to be the god Krishna in disguise. Krishna teaches the prince about his duty, and the right way to live and worship. This part of the poem is called the Bhagavad Gita. It is one of the best-loved parts of all Hindu holy books.

Bhagavad Gita means 'song of the Lord'. Some of the most difficult teachings of Hinduism are found in the Bhagavad Gita, but they are written in a way that people can understand easily. For many Hindus, the Bhagavad Gita is the most important of the Hindu holy books.

The Ramayana

The Ramayana was probably written down about 100 CE. It is divided into seven smaller books. In the Ramayana, the god Vishnu appears as Prince Rama.

The Ramayana tells the story of Prince Rama and his wife Sita. Sita is kidnapped by the wicked monster called Ravana. The monkey god Hanuman helps Prince Rama to find Sita and rescue her. Everything ends happily. Good wins over evil.

Understanding the stories

Hindus of different ages understand the stories of the Mahabharata and the Ramayana in different ways. For children, they are stories which are full of excitement. For adults, the stories teach very important things about the Hindu gods and about worship. Hindu actors and dancers often use these stories in their acts, because almost all Hindus know the stories and love them.

This old painting shows a scene from the Ramayana. Prince Rama and Sita are sitting down. Hanuman, the monkey god, kneels in front of them.

How to worship

Whoever offers me a leaf,
A flower, a fruit or water
    with devotion,
That offering I will accept
Because it was offered
    with love.
(From the Bhagavad Gita.)

Worship at home

Hindus believe that **Brahman** is in everything, so everything a Hindu does can be part of worship. Special worship is called **puja**.

Puja

Puja usually takes place in front of a **shrine**. In most Hindu homes, the shrine is in the mother's bedroom or in the kitchen. In some families, each person has their own shrine, with their own special gods. If the family can afford it, the shrine or shrines may be a whole room. The shrines usually have **images** and pictures of gods and goddesses, flowers and perfume. In other families, a shrine is small and simple.

In the home, it is usually the mother who makes puja. She may prepare for puja by having a bath and putting on clean clothes. The image of the god is then washed and dried. The mother may touch the image with coloured powders. Sometimes she wipes it with perfume, or hangs flowers from it.

This family is worshipping the elephant god Ganesha at their shrine.

This girl is worshipping the god Krishna. Notice that the image of Krishna is blue. Hindus believe this is a way of showing that something is holy.

During puja, small gifts are offered to the god. These are not large or expensive – perhaps only a grain of rice or a flower. What is important is that they are given with love.

Puja also includes repeating **mantras**. These are verses from the Hindu holy books, repeated over and over again. Hindus believe that this helps them to concentrate on Brahman. Mantras often begin with the holy word **Aum**. Sometimes the word Aum is used as a mantra on its own.

While they are making puja, Hindus do not wear shoes. They may stand, or they sit cross-legged. They often put their hands together and lift them up to their face, or put them in front of their chest. Sometimes they kneel and touch the ground with their forehead. These are all ways of showing respect to a god or goddess.

Hindu shrines
A Hindu shrine usually contains an image of the god or goddess which the family worships. There may be other images or pictures, too. There are flowers and perfume, so that the image and the pictures are surrounded by beauty. Sometimes there is a bottle of water from the River Ganga by the shrine. This river is sometimes called the Ganges in English. Hindus believe that the River Ganga is holy.

19

Hindu temples

In India, there are thousands of temples. Some are like small villages, with lots of buildings. Others are tiny **shrines** by the side of the road. In countries like the UK, some Hindu temples are built specially. More often, they are found in other buildings which have been changed so they can be used as a temple. Sometimes a temple is called a **mandir**, which is the word for temple in **Gujerati**, an Indian language.

▲ *These Hindus are worshipping at a small shrine by the side of a road in India.*

In India, temples are often built near a river. Hindus always wash themselves before worship. They also believe that rivers are holy. Temples may be at a place where the Hindu holy books say that something happened in the life of a god. Small shrines are often built at the side of the road. This may be to remember something that happened there, or to ask a god's protection for people who are travelling.

Carvings

Many temples have beautiful carvings, both inside and outside. These carvings often show parts of the story from the life of a Hindu god. The temple doorway is often 'guarded' by frightening creatures.

Inside a temple

At the entrance to a Hindu temple there is always a place where shoes can be left. Everyone going to worship removes their shoes as a mark of respect. This also shows that they are leaving the outside world behind them. It keeps the holy place clean, too.

The main room inside the temple is the shrine room. The shrine room usually has a carpet, and beautiful decorations, paintings and statues. There may also be other rooms in the temple where different gods can be worshipped.

Large temples have rooms where people can live. This is because many people may work in a temple, and they need somewhere to stay. A tiny shrine by the side of the road only has space for an **image** of a god and small things to help people worship.

The Aum symbol

*The most important sound for Hindus is the word **Aum** (sometimes spelled Om). It is said 'ah-oo-m'. Hindus believe this is a holy sound because it describes **Brahman**. Aum begins and ends all prayers and **mantras**, and is often used in worship.*

*The **symbol** Aum is often found on temple carvings and on objects used in Hindu worship.*

Worship in a temple

Worship often takes place in front of an image in a temple.

Hindus think of a temple as a place where a god can be visited. It is rather like a royal palace where a Hindu god or gods live.

Small temples have only one **image** of a god in one **shrine**. Large temples have more than one shrine. The biggest shrine has the image of the main god the temple is named after.

A temple always has at least one priest to look after the images of the gods. Most temples have at least one room where the priest lives. There is usually a river nearby, or another supply of water, so that people can wash themselves before they worship.

How do Hindus worship?

Worship in a temple usually begins before sunrise. The image of the god is 'woken up' by the priest, who says prayers. He washes the image in milk or water, then dries it. The priest may put a special perfumed paste on the image. The image is then dressed in clothes of red and gold, and has flowers placed around its neck. Hindus believe that every image should be worshipped at least once a day. In temples, the more important images are worshipped several times a day.

After the priest has made all the preparations, he draws back the curtains which are in front of the image. Hindus believe that at this moment they can see the image, and also that they can be 'seen' by **Brahman**. This is a very special moment which Hindus call **darshan**.

The arti ceremony

A special part of Hindu worship is called the **arti** ceremony. Small lights on a tray are offered to the god so that the god can bless them. The priest then carries the lights among the people who are worshipping. Sometimes they put small gifts of money on the tray. The people hold their hands over the flames, and then touch their eyes, forehead and head. They believe that by doing this they receive power from the god.

During the worship, people are given special food which they believe has been blessed by the god. It is called **prashad**. It is usually a mixture of nuts, fruits and sweets.

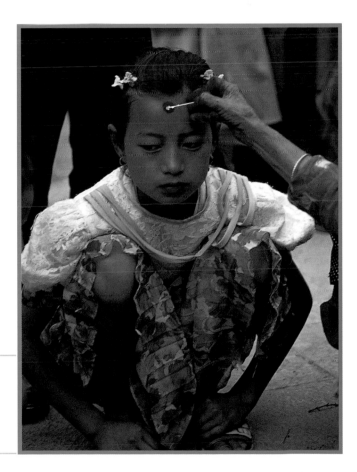

This girl is being given tilak, which shows that she has been to worship.

Tilak

*After worship, people may place a dot or stripes of a special powder or paste on their forehead. This is usually called **tilak**. The shape of the tilak shows which god the person has worshipped.*

Two important temples

The Pashupatinath temple in Nepal. This is a temple of the god Shiva.

The Pashupatinath temple, Nepal

Pashupatinath is an important place for Hindus to worship the god Shiva. The temple stands on the banks of the River Bagmati, about five kilometres outside Kathmandu, the capital of Nepal. The buildings which are there today go back to the seventeenth century CE. The place where they are built was used for worship for hundreds of years before that.

On the river bank there are many **ghats**. These are places where people bathe. They are also used for **cremations** after someone has died. The ghats which are closest to the front of the temple are only used for the cremations of members of the royal family.

A Hindu story

The Hindu holy books tell how some of the gods wanted to be able to live for ever. The god Vishnu told them to stir up the ocean to find the special liquid they needed. They stirred for a hundred years, and the ocean gave them many treasures. But then a great serpent under the sea began to spit out a deadly poison. The god Shiva leapt forward and swallowed the poison. By doing this, he saved the world. The poison could not harm Shiva because he was so powerful, but it stained his throat dark blue.

The main temple has three roofs which are covered in gold. Around the main temple are other buildings used by people who are worshipping and by the priests who live in the temple. There are many other smaller temples in the grounds of the main temple, too.

You can find the places mentioned in this book on the map on page 44.

The Shri Swaminarayan temple, London

This is the largest Hindu temple outside India. It was completed in 1995. The stone used to build it was carved in India. It was then brought to London and put together like a jigsaw puzzle. Because Hindus have great respect for life, everything in the temple was chosen carefully so as not to damage the Earth.

The temple has five beautifully carved **shrines** for the **images** of the gods. Worship takes place five times each day. The temple also has rooms which can be used for meetings and as classrooms. There is a hall where weddings can take place, and also a large sports hall.

▼ *The Shri Swaminarayan temple in London is the largest Hindu temple outside India.*

Pilgrimage

A **pilgrimage** is a journey which someone makes because of their religion. Most Hindus believe that by going on pilgrimage to a special place, they will achieve a better **karma**. Karma is the belief that actions in a person's past lives affect this life and future lives. Good actions in this life will help a person to be **reincarnated** to a better life next time.

Places of pilgrimage

You can find the places mentioned in this book on the map on page 44.

There are hundreds of places of pilgrimage all over India. The four most important places are thousands of kilometres apart, at the four 'corners' of India. Puri is on the east coast, Dwarka is on the west coast and Badrinath is in the far north of India. These are all **shrines** to the god Vishnu. Rameshwaram on the south coast is a shrine to the god Shiva. Many Hindus spend most of their lives saving money so they can visit all four of these places of pilgrimage.

When pilgrims visit shrines, worship there is similar to worship at any other time. At popular shrines, hundreds of people may queue for hours to gain **darshan** – the special moment when they see and are 'seen' by **Brahman**.

Worshippers at the temple at Puri, in eastern India.

People give presents to the god they have come to worship. These are the same things they would give at home, usually small gifts of food or flowers.

Varanasi (sometimes called Benares)

Varanasi is the most important place on the River Ganga, which Hindus believe is holy. Hindus believe that the god Shiva lived at Varanasi. It has been an important place of Hindu teaching for thousands of years.

Every Hindu hopes to be in Varanasi when they die. After dead bodies have been **cremated**, the ashes which are left are scattered in the River Ganga. The ashes of people who have died in other places are often scattered there, too. Hindus believe that this will help their **atman** to become part of Brahman.

The River Ganga

Hindus believe that the River Ganga in India (the River Ganges in English) is the holiest river in the world. Millions of Hindus bathe in its waters. They believe that drinking its water will get rid of all the wrong things they have done in this life and in previous lives.

▲ *A holy man bathing at the place where the River Ganga begins in the Himalayan mountains. Notice the ice in the background – it is the edge of the glacier.*

Celebrations – Divali

For most Hindus, Divali is the most important festival of the year. It takes place at the end of October or in November in the Western calendar. In different parts of India different stories are remembered at Divali. This means that the way the festival is celebrated often depends upon where a person lives.

Lighting candles is an important part of the celebrations for Divali.

Divas

Throughout Divali, Hindus decorate their homes, temples and other buildings with rows of lights. In the past, small clay lamps called **divas** were lit. Today, small electric lights like fairy lights are often used instead of lamps. Glitter and tinsel are often used for decorations, too.

Celebrating Divali

*At Divali people wear new or clean clothes, and give each other presents. They share meals with friends and family. Special patterns called **rangolis** are drawn on the floor with coloured powders. Hindus believe that this will bring good luck to the house. People often hold firework displays and bonfires, with singing and dancing. The loud bangs from the fireworks are believed to scare away evil.*

Remembering Lakshmi

For Hindus, Divali is a special time to remember Lakshmi, the goddess who brings good luck. Lakshmi is believed to visit houses which are clean and tidy. Some Hindus think that the divas and other decorations show her the way and welcome her to the house. At Divali, Hindus try to make up any quarrels they have had with people. It is a chance for a fresh new start. Hindus hope that Lakshmi will help the next year to be a good one.

Stories of Divali

The festival of Divali is an opportunity for Hindus to remember important stories from the holy books. In a story from the Ramayana, Prince Rama rescues his wife Sita. They return home and Prince Rama is crowned king. The people of the country are very pleased to see Prince Rama and Sita, and light lamps to line the streets to welcome them.

Other stories which Hindus remember at Divali tell how the god Vishnu wins a battle with a wicked giant. In another story, Vishnu outwits a powerful king named Bali.

Many of the stories of Divali remember Lakshmi, the goddess of good luck.

Celebrations – Navaratri and Dassehra

Navaratri

The festival of Navaratri takes place in the Indian month of Ashwin. This is September–October in the Western calendar. Navaratri lasts for nine nights. Like other Hindu festivals, different groups of Hindus remember different stories at Navaratri. Most of the celebrations remember the Mother Goddess. In this festival she is remembered as Durga, a fierce soldier who rides into battle on a lion.

People dance around a shrine to the goddess Durga at the festival of Navaratri.

In northern India, there are outdoor plays during the festival of Navaratri. They act out parts of the story from the Ramayana, part of the Hindu holy books.

In other places, people dance around a **shrine** to the goddess Durga. This shrine is a box with a cone-shaped top, and has different pictures of the goddess on each side. People dance and sing hymns to the goddess. Some people do this every night for nine nights! Hindus believe that they are given energy from the goddess, which they can use to fight evil.

Dassehra

Dassehra means 'tenth day'. The festival of Dassehra falls on the day after the end of the festival of Navaratri, which is nine nights long.

At the festival of Dassehra, an image of the goddess Durga is taken to the river to be washed.

During Dassehra **images** of the goddess Durga are taken to the nearest river and washed. Hindus believe that as the image disappears under the water it takes unhappiness and bad luck with it, and the river washes it all away. This makes Dassehra a very happy festival.

During the festival, Hindus also remember the story from the Ramayana about how Prince Rama prayed to the goddess Durga for help before he fought a battle against the wicked Ravana. Statues of Ravana are burned on bonfires. In New Delhi, the capital of India, wooden statues of Ravana and his two brothers are built 30 metres high. They are packed with fireworks and burnt.

The meaning of the festivals

Hindu festivals are times for people to meet and enjoy themselves, and for families and friends to be together. There is dancing and special food. There are important lessons, too. Stories like the ones from the Ramayana remind people of **Brahman's** *love. In the stories, good always wins over evil, and this reminds people that they should live a good life.*

Celebrations – Holi and Raksha Bandhan

A procession celebrating Holi. Notice that the people are all covered in coloured powder!

Holi

The festival of Holi is celebrated by Hindus all over the world. It takes place in the Indian month of Phalguna. This is February–March in the Western calendar.

Many stories which Hindus tell at Holi are about the god Krishna. Hindus believe that when Krishna was young he often used to play tricks on people. Because of this, Holi is a time for practical jokes. A favourite trick with children is to throw coloured powders and water over people in the streets. This remembers Krishna's friendship with a group of milkmaids. In one story from the Hindu holy books Krishna's favourite milkmaid, Radha, threw coloured dye over Krishna when they went out for a walk. Hindus believe that this story has a religious meaning. It shows how well Krishna and Radha got on together, and it reminds people that they must love **Brahman**.

How Holi got its name

The festival of Holi gets its name from a more serious Hindu story. Once there was a king who thought he was very important. He wanted everyone to worship him as a god. His son, Prahlada, knew that this was wrong, and he refused. Twice, the wicked king tried to kill his son. Both times, the god Vishnu saved Prahlada.

The third time, the king asked his equally wicked daughter, Holika, to help. She took Prahlada with her to the top of a huge bonfire. She had special powers, and she thought that she would be safe, but that her brother would die. Again, Vishnu saved Prahlada. Holika's powers failed, and she was destroyed. Holi is named after Holika.

Raksha Bandhan

The festival of Raksha Bandhan takes place in July–August, in the Indian month of Shravan. Raksha Bandhan is a festival for brothers and sisters. Raksha means 'protection' and Bandhan means 'tie'. At Raksha Bandhan, a girl ties a bracelet called a **rakhi** around her brother's wrist. The rakhi is made of coloured silk or cotton. She says a short prayer asking the gods to look after him in the year ahead. Then she gives him a sweet. In return, the brother gives her a present, and he promises to look after her and protect her.

A girl ties a rakhi around her brother's wrist.

Why do girls give a bracelet?
A Hindu story tells that the god Indra fought with a wicked king called Bali. Indra lost the battle, so Indra's wife asked Vishnu to help. Vishnu gave her a bracelet made of cotton threads to tie around Indra's wrist. The bracelet had special powers, so Indra won the battle.

33

Celebrations – other festivals

There are many different Hindu festivals throughout the year. Some festivals are important in a particular area, or to Hindus who worship a particular god. Most festivals involve making **puja**.

Mahashivaratri

Mahashivaratri is a serious festival which remembers the god Shiva. It takes place in the Indian month of Phalguna, which is January–February in the Western calendar. Hindus believe that Shiva performs a special dance which provides the energy that keeps the universe moving. Mahashivaratri means 'great night of Shiva', and Hindus believe that this is the night he dances his special dance.

These Hindus are celebrating Mahashivaratri.

Fasting for festivals

*Many Hindu festivals are a time of **fasting**. Fasting often means going without food and drink altogether, but for Hindus it means going without certain foods. For example, when they are fasting they do not eat foods such as meat, fish, onions, garlic, rice, wheat and beans. Foods which are allowed on fast days are things such as fresh fruit, milk and **ghee**.*

At Mahashivaratri, **images** of Shiva are very important. Many images of Shiva show him dancing. He has three lines across his forehead, and people who worship him have these on their foreheads, too. A **symbol** of Shiva is the **linga**. This is a stone column. As part of their worship at Mahashivaratri, Hindus pour milk over a linga.

Janmashtami

The festival of Janmashtami takes place in the Indian month of Shravan, which is July–August in the Western calendar. Janmashtami celebrates the birthday of the god Krishna. Stories from the Hindu holy books say that Krishna was born at midnight, so many Hindus spend all night in the temple. They dance and sing songs praising Krishna. At midnight, everyone makes puja in front of the **shrine** which holds an image of the baby Krishna. They share **prashad**, which are special foods which they believe have been blessed by the god. They drink a special sweet drink made of milk, yoghurt, sugar, water and honey.

In many temples at Janmashtami, there are non-stop repeated readings of the Bhagavad Gita, part of the Hindu holy books, for the eight days and nights before the festival. It takes about three hours to read the Bhagavad Gita all the way through. People take it in turns, and the readings are timed so that they finish at midnight on Krishna's birthday.

These decorations are for Janmashtami, Krishna's birthday.

Special occasions – childhood

Samskars are special ceremonies which are held at sixteen different times during every Hindu's life. They happen at times when there is some sort of change. Hindus believe that at these times a person might be at risk from evil. Samskars are intended to protect him or her.

The first three samskars happen before a baby is born. They are prayers that **Brahman** will protect the mother and the baby. The fourth samskar happens when the baby is born. The baby is washed, and the father or a priest places a few drops of honey in the baby's mouth, using a gold ring. He says, 'May your life be as precious as gold.'

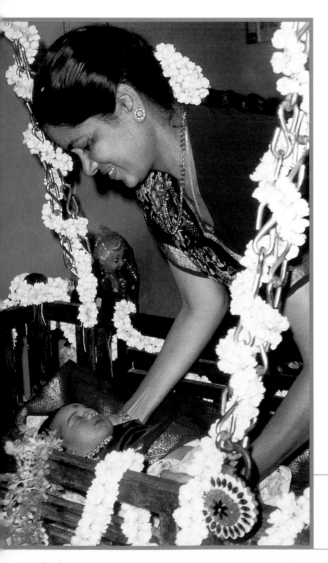

The naming ceremony (fifth samskar)

The fifth samskar is the naming ceremony. The baby is usually given its name when it is twelve days old. He or she is dressed in new clothes, and placed in a cradle. The baby's name is said out loud by the eldest woman in the family. The father says into the baby's ear, 'Now your name is ...' The baby's friends and family sing songs, and eat a special sweet made of fruit, nuts and sugar.

The next three samskars happen as the baby grows. The ninth samskar happens at the time of the baby's first hair-cut, usually around the age of one.

A Hindu baby is placed in a cradle before the naming ceremony.

A baby boy has his head shaved. This is a way of showing that any bad things from lives he has lived before have been taken away.

The thread ceremony (tenth samskar)

The tenth samskar is called the thread ceremony. It is a very important ceremony for boys who belong to the three higher **varnas**. At the time of the tenth samskar, the boy is usually between seven and twelve years old. A loop of cotton is placed over his left shoulder, hanging down to his right hip. This thread shows that he is joining the Hindu religion. The boy wears this for the rest of his life, changing it at festivals. After the ceremony, there is a meal for family and friends, and the boy is given presents.

▲ A Hindu teacher prepares a boy for the thread ceremony.

Horoscopes

*Many Hindus use **horoscopes** when they make plans. They believe that a horoscope tells the future, based on the position of the stars in the sky. Hindus' horoscopes are always written by a priest. He uses information about the person's birth and about his or her parents. The horoscope tells the person which days are likely to be good ones to choose for important events such as weddings.*

Special occasions – marriage

Hindus believe that marriage is important, so there can be children to carry on the family. Hindu marriages are usually 'arranged'. This means that parents and older relatives choose or suggest a suitable husband or wife. In the past, couples did not meet until their wedding day. Today, things are not usually so strict. The young person may suggest a possible partner, or they may meet the chosen person a few times before they marry.

The wedding

A Hindu wedding itself usually lasts about one hour, but a number of the celebrations may go on for several days. The bride wears special make-up, a new red and gold **sari**, and lots of gold jewellery. Preparing her for the wedding takes several hours. The bridegroom also makes special **puja** to prepare him for the wedding. Both the bride and bridegroom wear flowers around their neck.

The couple sit in front of a special fire. This is a **symbol** that **Brahman** is there with them. Their right hands are tied together, and holy water is sprinkled on them. There are prayers and offerings of rice. The couple walk carefully around the fire saying prayers.

An outdoor Hindu wedding in India.

They take seven steps together near the fire. Each step has a special meaning. The seven steps stand for food, strength, wealth, happiness, children, the seasons and lasting friendship. At each step they stop and make promises to each other. While they do this, they are joined by a piece of cloth, which shows that they are being joined as husband and wife. After she is married, the bride becomes part of her husband's family.

Divorce

Divorce means ending a marriage while a husband and wife are still alive. Divorce is allowed in Indian law, but strict Hindus do not accept divorce. It is seen as a disgrace to both families if the couple divorce.

▲ *During a Hindu wedding, the couple pray and make offerings to a god.*

Ashramas

*Hindus believe that a man's life is divided into four stages, called **ashramas**. The first ashrama is called the student. The second ashrama is called the householder. The third stage is called the forest-dweller. At this stage, a man should go and live alone in a peaceful place. This prepares him for the last stage, which is called a holy man. A holy man has no home and spends all his time thinking and praying. Today, not everyone follows these stages.*

Special occasions – death and reincarnation

Reincarnation

Hindus believe in **reincarnation**. This is the belief that when a person's body dies, the **soul** – called the **atman** – moves on to another being. This may be another person, a plant or an animal. Hindus believe that the atman in everything is the same. When a person dies their atman is reborn. This happens over and over again, until the atman becomes completely pure (holy). Then it can go back to being part of **Brahman**, where it began. This is what Hindus aim for.

Where the atman is reborn depends on how a person has lived in this life. This is called the law of **karma**. Karma means 'action'. A good karma in a person's previous life will mean they have a good life this time. A bad karma in the person's previous life will mean they have a hard life this time.

Hindu funerals

When someone dies, their body is washed and wrapped in a cloth. Flowers may be placed on the cloth. The body is then taken to be **cremated** on a **funeral pyre**. This may be built on a **ghat** (platform) by a river. In Indian cities, and in countries such as the UK, bodies are taken to a crematorium.

A funeral procession through a town in India.

The eldest son or closest male relative walks around the funeral pyre three times carrying a lighted torch. Then he lights the fire. **Ghee** is used to help the fire burn. Some families burn a special sweet-smelling wood on the fire, too. The people say prayers, and there are readings from the Hindu holy books to remind people that everyone who dies will be reborn. The closest male relative stays until the fire has gone out, then he collects the ashes which remain.

After the funeral

After the funeral the relatives return home and bathe. They do not go out and meet people until all the ceremonies are over. The last ceremony is the kriya ceremony.

All Hindus hope that they will be in the city of Varanasi when they die, and that their ashes will be scattered on the River Ganga. They believe that this will save them many future rebirths. Hindus living in other countries may have a relative's ashes flown back to India so they can be scattered on the River Ganga.

The kriya ceremony
This ceremony takes place ten or twelve days after a funeral. Rice and milk are made into offerings. After this, Hindus believe that the person's atman has been reborn.

You can find the places mentioned in this book on the map on page 44.

Ashes left after cremation are often scattered on the River Ganga.

Ways to be a Hindu

The four aims of life

Hindus believe that every person has their own **dharma**. Dharma means 'duty'. Dharma includes things such as worship, doing one's best at work, and not hurting other people or animals. Dharma is different for everyone because it depends on the person, their background, which **jati** they belong to and many other things.

Doing their dharma to the best of their ability is the first aim in life for Hindus. The second aim is to be able to provide for their family. The third aim is to be able to enjoy good things in life without hurting other people or themselves in any way. The fourth aim is to break out of the cycle of **reincarnation**. These four aims are a very important part of life for every Hindu.

Part of each person's dharma is to choose the way they worship. The Bhagavad Gita mentions four 'paths' which people may use in their worship. Hindus can follow more than one path, or different ones at different times in their life. The important thing is that the path they choose leads to freedom from rebirth.

Deciding how to worship is part of each person's dharma.

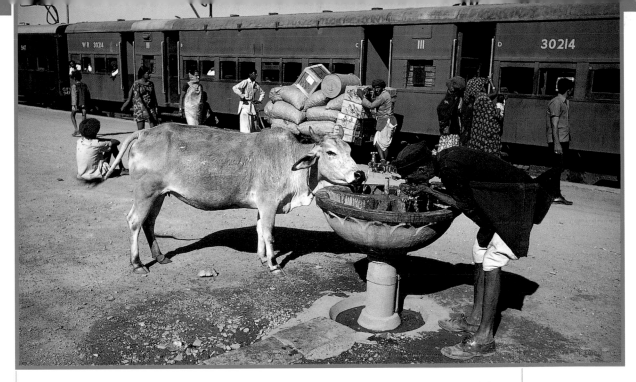

▲ *In India, cows are allowed to wander wherever they like.*

Respect for life

Hindus believe that the **atman** in everything is the same, so they try to be kind to all living things. Many Hindus do not eat meat at all. No Hindu eats beef. Everywhere in India, the cow is treated as holy. Cows are milked and their dung is used as fertilizer and as fuel, but they are never harmed. They wander where they like, even in towns and cities. If someone kills or injures a cow, they can be put in prison.

In the world

There are Hindus in many countries across the world. The teaching about dharma means that education is very important to them. Hindus living in rich countries often send money to their family or friends who live in poorer places.

The Brihadaranyaka Upanishad

These words from the holy books sum up how Hindus try to live:

From the unreal
   lead me to the real
From the darkness
   lead me to light
From death
   lead me to immortality.

Map

The map below shows places that are mentiond in this book. They are some of the places that are important in the history of Hinduism.

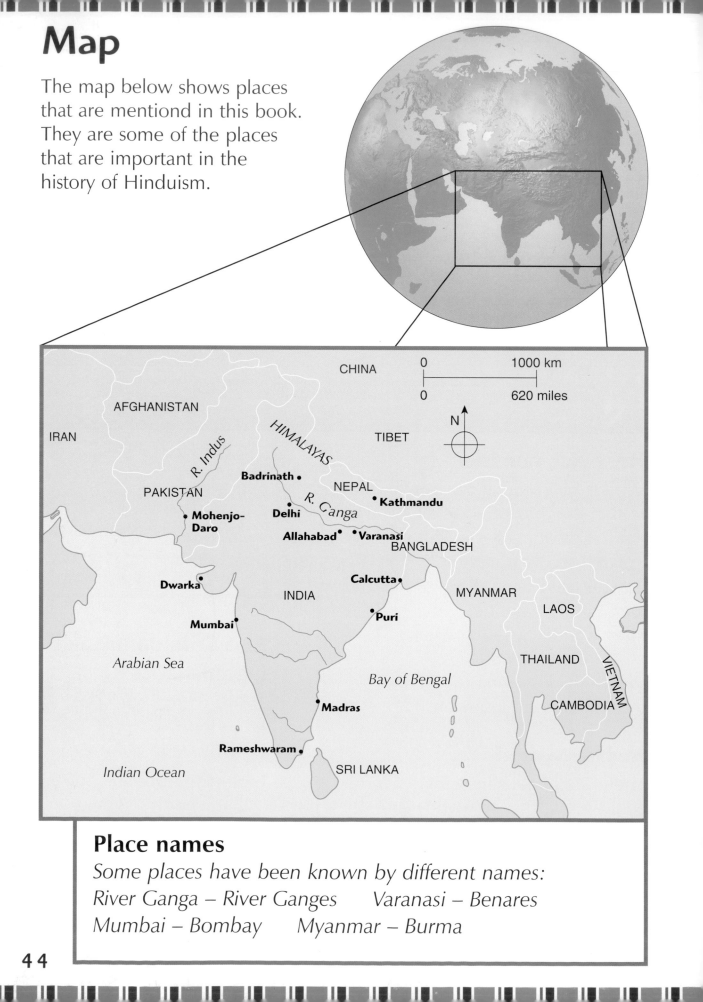

Place names

Some places have been known by different names:
River Ganga – River Ganges   Varanasi – Benares
Mumbai – Bombay   Myanmar – Burma

Timechart

Major events in World history

BCE	3000–1700	Indus valley civilization (Hinduism)
	c2685–1196	Egyptian civilization
	c2000	Abraham lived (Judaism)
	1800	Stonehenge completed
	c528	Siddhattha Buddha born (Buddhism)
	c450–146	Greek Empire
	200	Great Wall of China begun
	c300–300CE	Roman Empire
	c4	Jesus of Nazareth born (Christianity)
CE	570	Muhammad born (Islam)
	1066	Battle of Hastings and the Norman conquest of England
	1325–1521	Aztec Empire
	1400	Black Death kills one person in three in China, North Africa and Europe
	1469	Guru Nanak born (Sikhism)
	1564	William Shakespeare born
	1914–18	World War I
	1939–45	World War II
	1946	First computer invented
	1969	First moon landings
	2000	Millennium celebrations all over the world

Major events in Hindu history

BCE	3000–1700	Indus Valley civilization (people worship nature gods)
	1500	Aryans invaders (people worship gods of sun and moon)
	1200	Beginning of the stories of the Vedas
	400–200	Upanishads written down
	c300	Mahabharata first written down
	c100	Ramayana first written down
CE	300	Laws of Manu written down
	500	Puranas first written down
	1400	Vedas written down
	1834–1886	Ramakrishna (Hindu leader and teacher)
	1869–1948	Mahatma Gandhi
	1947	Indian independence

Glossary

ahimsa	fighting without using violence
arti	worship of Brahman through fire
ashrama	one of the four stages of life
atman	the soul which Hindus believe is in everything
Aum	sacred sound and symbol for Hindus
Brahman	Hindu name for the Great Power
Brahmins	highest of the four varnas
Buddhist	follower of the Buddha Gotama and Buddhism
caste	group in Indian society
cremation	burning a dead body
darshan	'see' – the moment of contact between Brahman and the person who worships
dharma	'duty' – the first aim in life for Hindus
diva	small clay lamp used at the festival of Divali
eternal	lasting for ever
fast	go without certain foods
funeral pyre	fire used for cremation
ghat	platform by a river used for worship or cremation
ghee	special kind of butter (clarified butter)
Gujerati	language used in India
Harijan	the lowest jati
horoscope	way of telling the future based on the position of the stars
image	statue used by Hindus in worship
jati	group in Hindu society
karma	'action' – actions in this life which affect future lives
Kshatriya	second of the four varnas

linga	stone column which is a symbol of the god Shiva
mandir	Gujerati name for a Hindu place of worship
mantra	repeated prayer
Moghul	Muslim ruler of India
Muslim	follower of the religion of Islam
pilgrimage	journey made for religious reasons
prashad	food which has been blessed by a god
puja	worship
rakhi	bracelet given to a boy by his sister at the festival of Raksha Bandhan
rangoli	pattern drawn in coloured powder or chalk
reincarnation	belief that the soul is reborn
samskars	the sixteen ceremonies to mark different stages of life
Sanatan dharma	eternal truths (name for Hinduism)
Sanskrit	very old Indian language
sari	long piece of material worn as a dress
shrine	holy place
shruti	'heard' – name for some of the Hindu holy books
Shudras	lowest of the four varnas
smriti	'remembered' – name for some of the Hindu holy books
soul	part of a person which lives on after their death
symbol	something that stands for something else
tilak	powder mark placed on the forehead to show that a Hindu has been to worship
trance	state between being unconscious and being awake
varna	four groups in Indian society
Vaishyas	third of the four varnas
Vedas	Hindu holy books

Index

Titles in the *Religions of the World* series include:

Hardback   0 431 14953 4

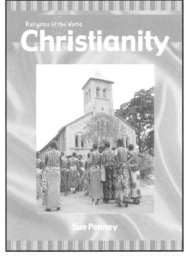

Hardback   0 431 14950 X

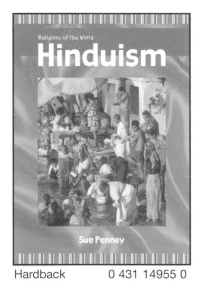

Hardback   0 431 14955 0

Hardback   0 431 14952 6

Hardback   0 431 14954 2

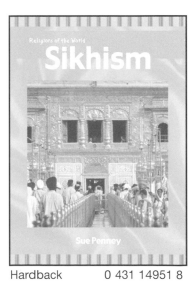

Hardback   0 431 14951 8

Find out about the other titles in this series on our website www.heinemann.co.uk/library